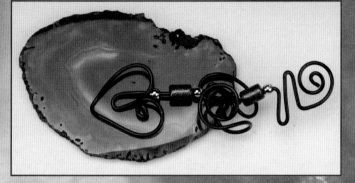

Beads & Agate Jewelry

to create yourself

Connie Wagner

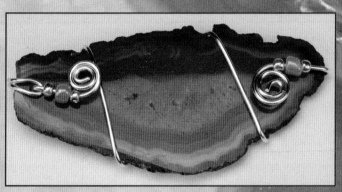

Schiffer Publishing Ltd

4880 Lower Valley Road, Atglen, Pa 19310

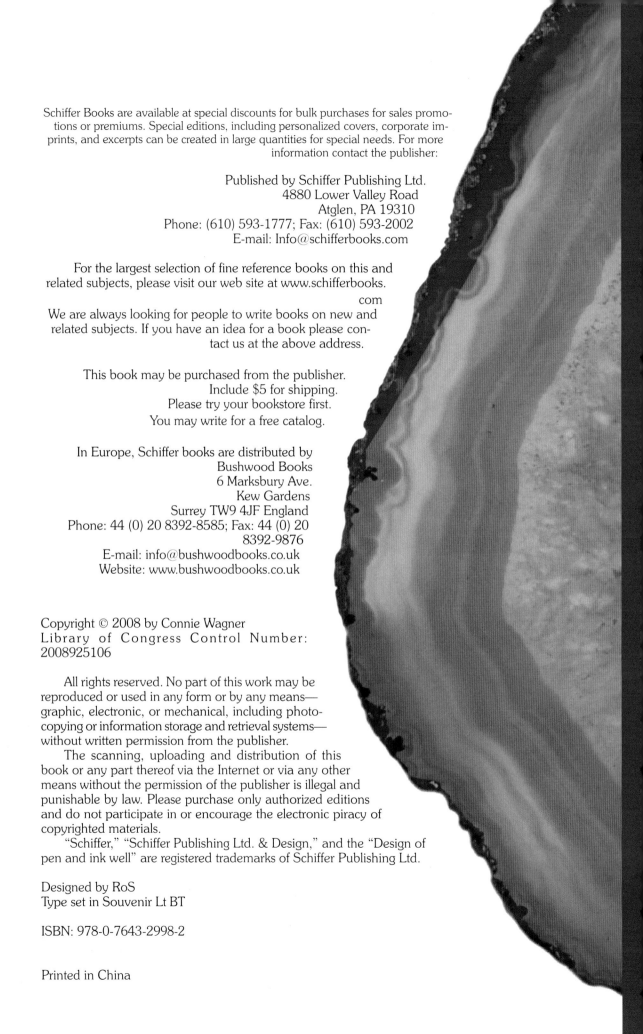

Schiffer Books are available at special discounts for bulk purchases for sales promotions or premiums. Special editions, including personalized covers, corporate imprints, and excerpts can be created in large quantities for special needs. For more information contact the publisher:

Published by Schiffer Publishing Ltd.
4880 Lower Valley Road
Atglen, PA 19310
Phone: (610) 593-1777; Fax: (610) 593-2002
E-mail: Info@schifferbooks.com

For the largest selection of fine reference books on this and related subjects, please visit our web site at www.schifferbooks.com
We are always looking for people to write books on new and related subjects. If you have an idea for a book please contact us at the above address.

This book may be purchased from the publisher.
Include $5 for shipping.
Please try your bookstore first.
You may write for a free catalog.

In Europe, Schiffer books are distributed by
Bushwood Books
6 Marksbury Ave.
Kew Gardens
Surrey TW9 4JF England
Phone: 44 (0) 20 8392-8585; Fax: 44 (0) 20 8392-9876
E-mail: info@bushwoodbooks.co.uk
Website: www.bushwoodbooks.co.uk

Designed by RoS
Type set in Souvenir Lt BT

ISBN: 978-0-7643-2998-2

Printed in China

Contents

Dedication   *4*

Acknowledgments   *4*

Introduction   *5*

Project 1. Agate Earrings   *8*

Project 2. Agate Barrette   *16*

Project 3. Agate Pin   *24*

Project 4. Agate Necklace   *34*

A Gallery of Agate Projects   *52*

Resources   *64*

Dedication

To my mother, "I can't believe I did it first."
To my children, for without them I would never be where I am today.
To my husband, for being supportive when I need him. Thank you.

Acknowledgments

I thank the Schiffer family and publishing team for helping me make this book.

Introduction

The projects in this book are created with agate stones, wire, and beads. Agates are chalcedony quartz. I use 18-gauge wire because it is moveable to create your design, at the same time it holds the design firmly.

I use the sliced form of agate. With this form you can have a large variety of designs; no two agates are ever alike. Some have a symmetrical design coming from the center, others have a liner pattern going across, and some just have their own personality of pattern.

Every agate has a different sense of translucence. Some are as clear as glass, but others are so opaque you can't see the sun through them. Also, as the projects in this book relate to jewelry, the color depends on what color clothing is worn with them; it will affect the stone's color. You will see a variety of agates here, with their variety of colors, shapes, sizes, and designs.

Agates got their name from the Achate River region of southwestern Sicily. They are found throughout the world and some agate varieties have become known by the name of the region in which they were first discovered (Brazilian, Botswana, etc.). They retain the name even when they are found elsewhere. Agates are formed when gas bubbles are trapped in solidifying lava and then become filled with alkali and silica-bearing water, which coagulates into a gel. The alkali attacks iron in the surrounding lava and bands of the resulting iron hydroxide are created in the gel. The gel loses moisture and crystallizes, leaving the bands intact. Many forms of agate are known, but all began the same way.

The stones I use are agates shipped in through Brazil. These are colored agates I order through a shipper in Connecticut. They are ¼" thick. I order them through a website: Pelham-grayson.com

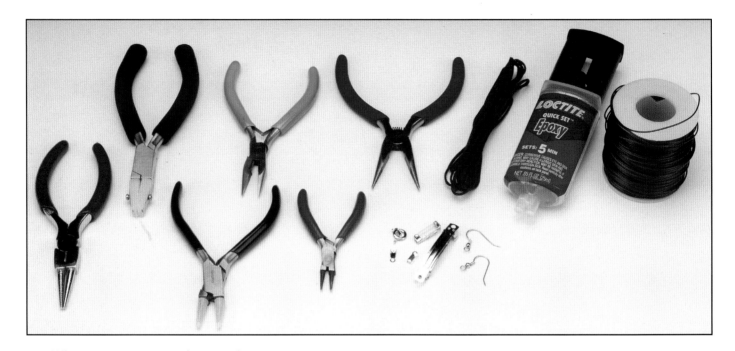

When you start using these tools on the colored para-wire, you have to learn how tightly to hold the pliers. If you hold them too tight you will chip the paint off the wire, but if you hold them too loose you will not get the design as tight as you want. If you do chip the paint, you can incorporate the mistake in the design by covering it up with other wire or beads, or you may have to redo the piece. I suggest practicing the techniques on non-colored wire, such as gold, brass, and silver.

The projects are jewelry, but you can use these techniques, patterns, and ideas on any agate piece to create an art object. You might make figures, sun catchers, bookmarks, keychains, as well as anything else you can think of. Be creative.

To begin any agate project, I have to get into a certain frame of mind. It is time to get work done, but I'm creating something beautiful from natural materials, so I try to enhance and not take away from its beauty. When I pick up an agate, I consider the following thoughts for creating jewelry:

I will be using a combination of glass, metal, and plastic beads in large and small sizes. They measure from 1/8" up to ¾". These can be found anywhere at any craft store.

Left: Here are the tools that will be used in the projects. 18 gauge colored copper wire (it holds up well), epoxy glue for stone, glass, and metal, cotton cord for the necklace (1.5 mm), two needle nosed pliers (smooth and ridged for grip), three round needle nosed pliers (small, large, and with plastic coating), flat nosed pliers mounted with rubber tips (the rubber tips keep you from ripping the coating off the copper wire), barrette backs, pin backs, 9mm string ring clasps, crimp end connectors, and earrings hooks.

1) Which side is the front, and what is the top of the stone? As you're turning the agate in your hands, think about what position will show its beauty best.

2) Do you see something in the agate—a face, a sunset, a silhouette of something? If you do, use it in your design.

3) Think about the shape of the agate. Examples are: if it's a teardrop, you may want to accent it with wire, beads, or another agate at the top or bottom. If it shows a landscape scene, you may want to present it horizontally.

4) What color wire will best work with the agate? If there has a little of another color hiding in it, I use that color wire to accent the agate. You can use black to outline the form or silver to add sparkle.

5) Are you going to use the wire within the design?
What wire design will work best with the piece? Does it need to be simple, because the design in the agate is strong enough to stand alone, or does it need help with wire? I do fancy wire designs because the agate doesn't have enough pizzazz on its own. You can frame the agate, as I did in the necklace in this book, or you can make a partial frame, maybe only three loops on the outside of the piece to accent it. This type of design is seen in some of the gallery pieces.

6) Does the agate need beads to accent it? Are you going to do the beads symmetrically, assymetrically, all mixed up, or have just one or two beads?
All of these ideas are seen in the gallery.

7) Do you need more than one agate to complete the piece?
Look at the design in the agates—will they complement each other? Does it look like one agate's lines are dripping into the other? Is one a landscape, and you could add another above it as a sun. Could the top one be a bell, and the lower, smaller one be the ringer? Be creative. You could combine two agates for a necklace or a larger piece, as shown in the gallery at the back of this book.

Project 1
Agate Earrings

The completed Agate Earrings Project.

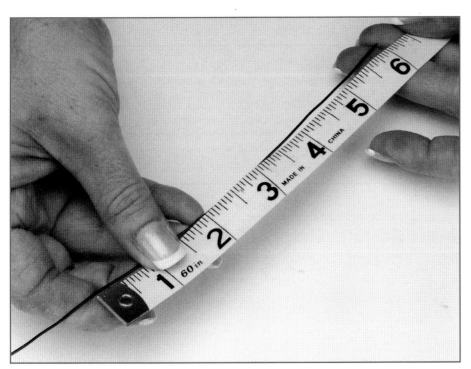

The first project is earrings. Begin by cutting six inches of blue wire using the wire cutting attachment to the needle nosed pliers. Cut two 6-inch lengths.

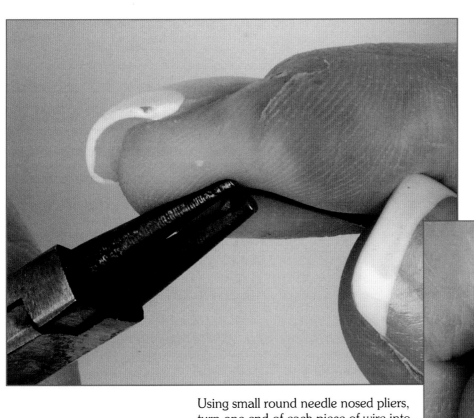

Using small round needle nosed pliers, turn one end of each piece of wire into a small loop. Since you're making a pair of earrings, repeat each step twice, once for each earring, as you go. That way you won't have to retrace your steps for the second earring.

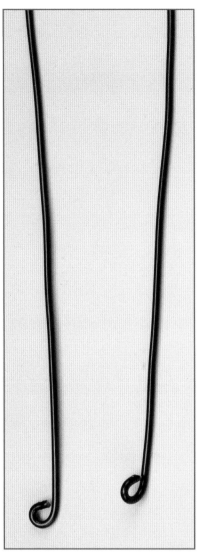

The loops
are in place.

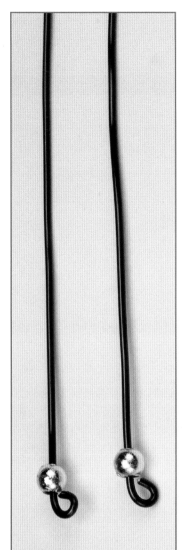

Slide a bead onto
each of the two
pieces of wire. I like
to choose wire colors
and beads that will
complement the
stones I'm using for
each project.

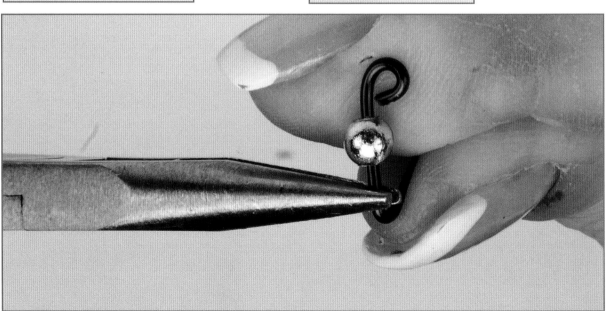

Bend the wire roughly ¼"
from the curled end at a right
angle.

Here's the stone we will be using. Buy stones that come with pre-drilled holes (2mm in diameter) to save yourself some time and effort.

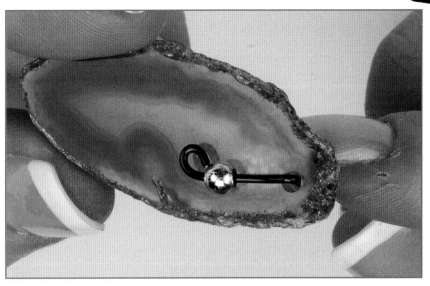

Thread the wire through the hole in the stone up to the bend.

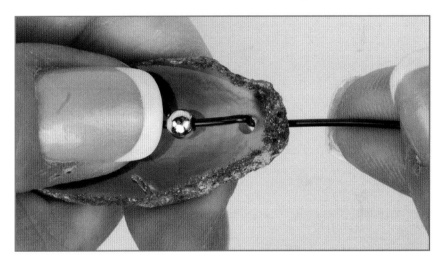

Now, hold the beaded end of the wire against the stone, and bend the wire behind the stone up against the back of the stone.

Now bend the wire that extends behind the stone up and over the front of the stone.

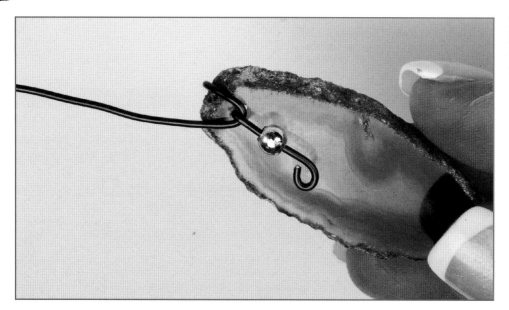

Now loop the wire behind the beaded end of the wire, pulling the long length of wire back away from the stone.

Using the rubber tipped pliers, squeeze the lengths of wire together to secure them. Be gentle so as not to chip the paint coating the wire.

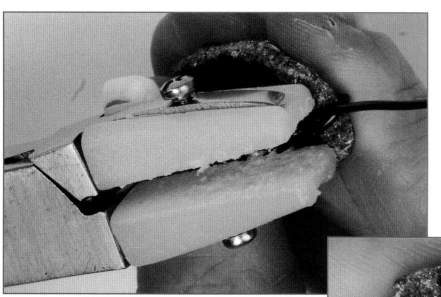

Use your thumb to curl the wire back around toward the stone in a gentle arc.

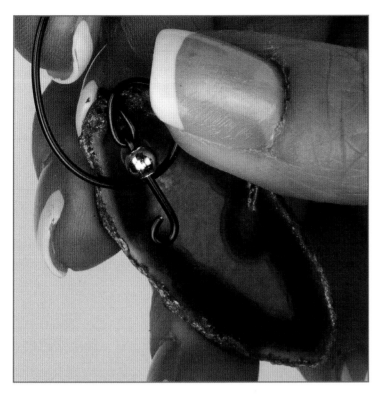

Bring the curved wire all the way around, under the beaded end again, to create a circle.

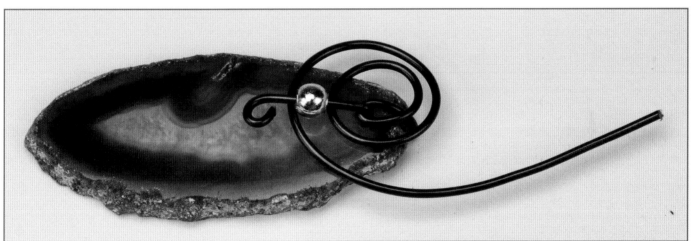

Repeat the curving process to create a second circle.

Bring the loose end back around and up through the back of the first circle you created.

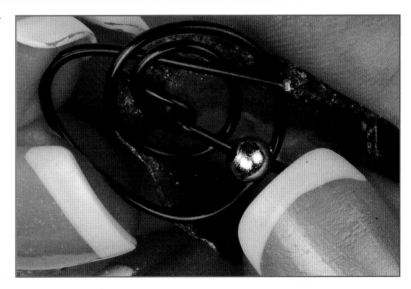

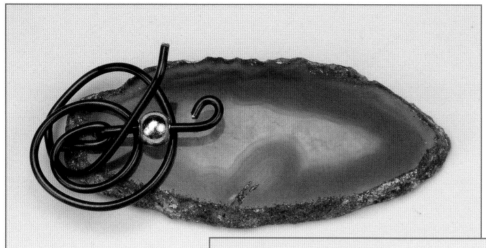

Pull the wire through tight without crimping the two circles you created.

Add two beads to the loose end of the wire. I have chosen silver beads because the complement the stone. You can choose whatever colors you feel best work with the stone colors you choose.

Now curl the loose end of the wire as you did at the very beginning to close off that length of wire in an attractive manner.

Flatten the rough end of the loop down against the wire so that the sharp, cut end cannot catch on anything later.

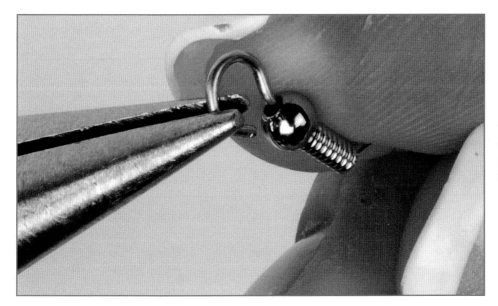

To attach the earring clasps, use small needle nosed pliers (smooth) to open up the end of the loop slightly for attachment.

Hook the earring clasp loop through the top loop of the earring.

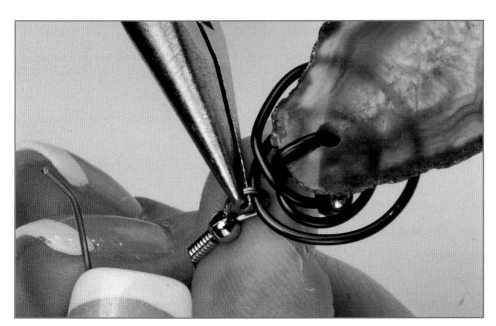

Use the needle nosed pliers to close the end of the earring clasps. This completes the Agate Earrings Project.

Project 2
Agate Barrette

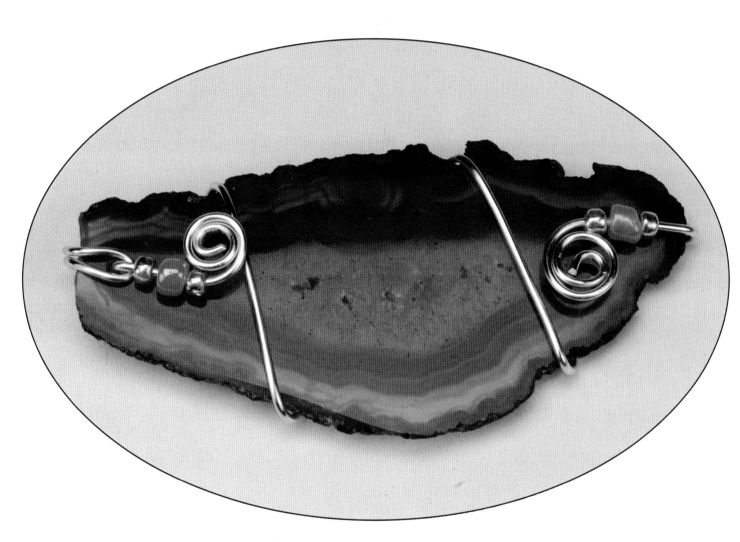

The completed Agate Barrette Project.

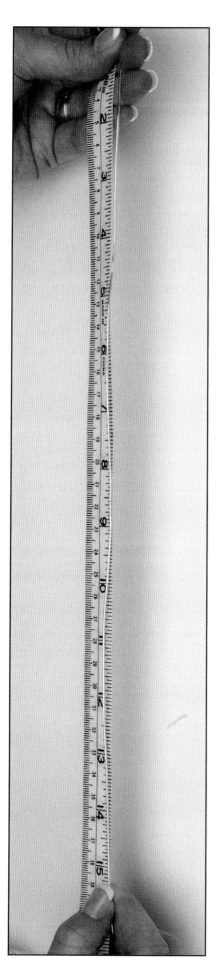

Take 15" of wire to start.

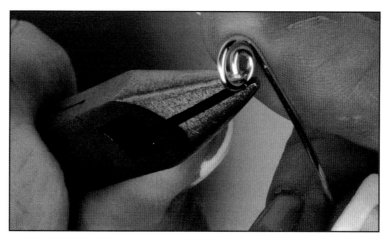

Using flat nosed needle nosed pliers, begin looping one end of the wire. When you reach a certain point, about two loops in, you'll need to switch to flat rubber nosed pliers.

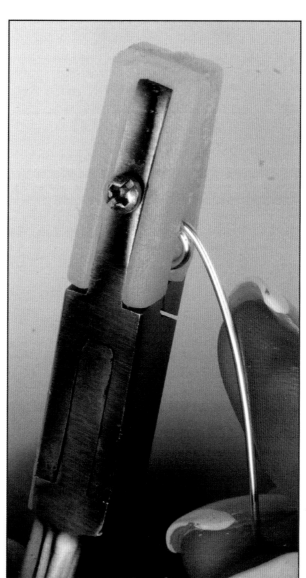

Finish the second of two loops with the flat rubber nosed pliers.

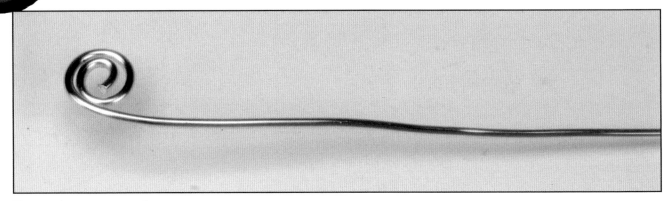

The two loops are complete.

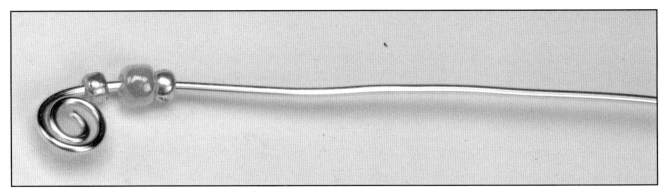

String three beads to the looped end of the wire.

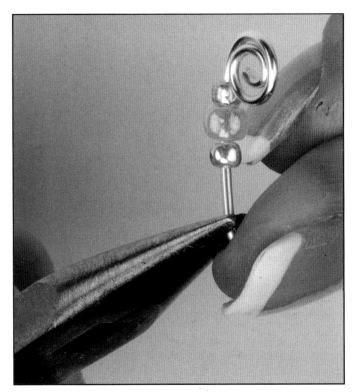

Bend the wire beyond the beads at a 45 degree angle.

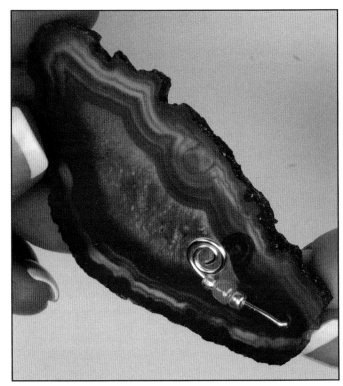

Run the wire through the stone up to the bend in the wire. For any piece in which wire will be wound around the stone, I used stones with rough edges to better hold the wire in place.

Bring the wire up from behind the stone, loop it under the angled wire on the front of the stone, and crimp it tight with the needle nosed pliers to hold it all in place.

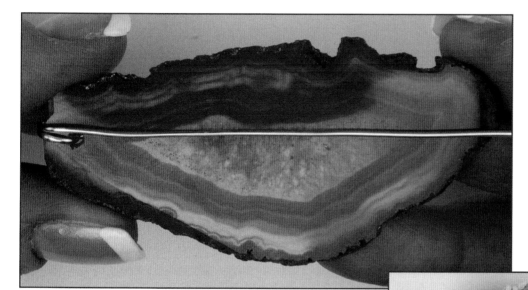

Now bend the wire back behind the stone.

Bend the wire with the pliers toward the first indent in the stone. The shape of the stone and the placement of the indents in it will dictate the way the wire is wrapped around the body of the stone.

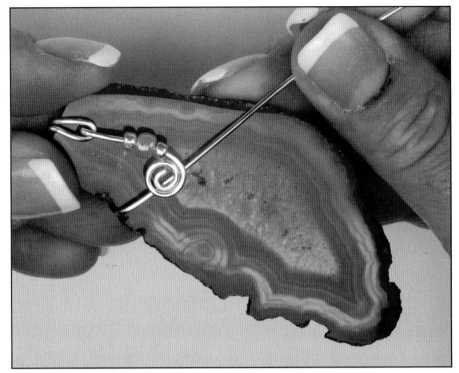

Bring the wire back around to the front of the stone and cross the face of the stone to the other side. Pick a point on the other side to wrap the wire around behind, a place that will support the wire and keep it from slipping when you are finished. This wide spot is a perfect place to wrap the wire.

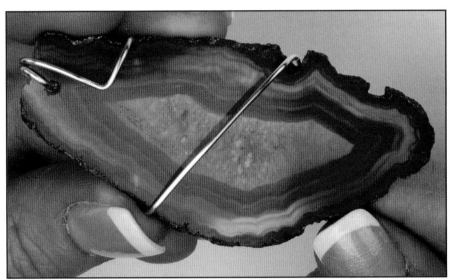

Wrapping the wire around behind the stone and back through the second large notch in the side of the stone. This is a terrific spot to bring the wire around front again.

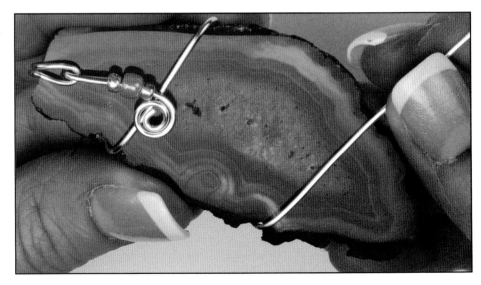

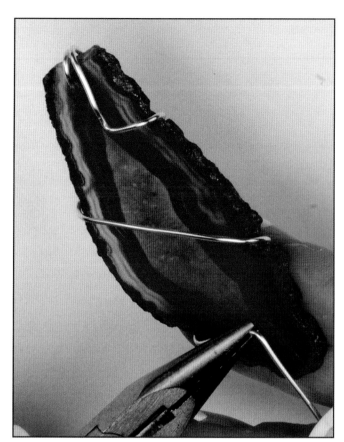

Wrap the wire around behind again and crimp the wire at an angle toward the top of the stone, just as you did at the beginning of the project.

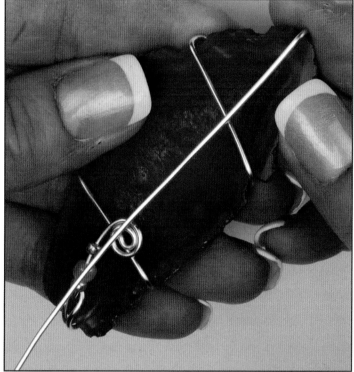

Bring the wire back around to the front of the stone, over the very tip. Press tight with your finger as the wire comes over the top to make sure it is a tight fit to the stone.

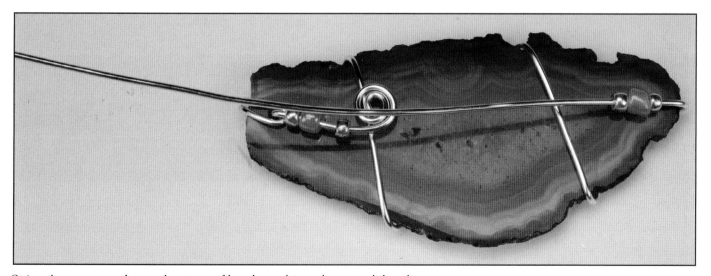

String the same number and pattern of beads on this end as you did at the start.

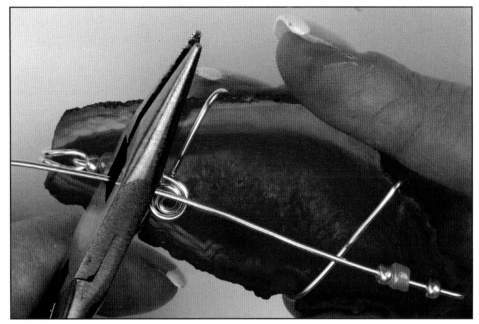

If you discover you've used too much wire, as I have, just cut off the excess with the wire cutter. I want the spiral at this end to match the spiral I made first. Using the flat nosed needle nosed pliers, create the spiral again, working in the opposite direction. Make sure the spirals are flat. You don't want any ends to snag on clothing or on skin.

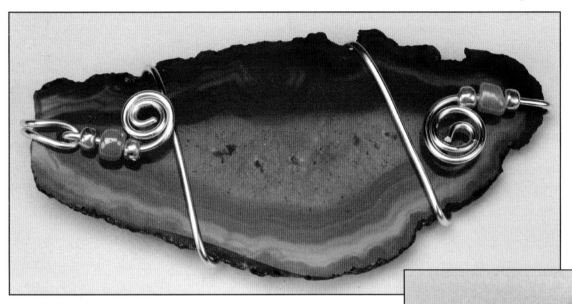

Now mix your Epoxy and spread the glue on the back of the barrette clasp. Use only materials you wish to throw away (paper plates, Popsicle sticks, etc.) when mixing and applying Epoxy.

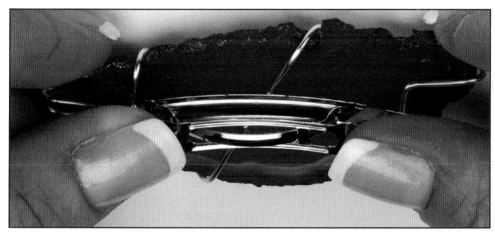

Attach the barrette clasp to the back of the stone and hold it firmly in place. You can offset the clasp a bit so it comes in contact with more of the stone surface so it will have a tighter grip.

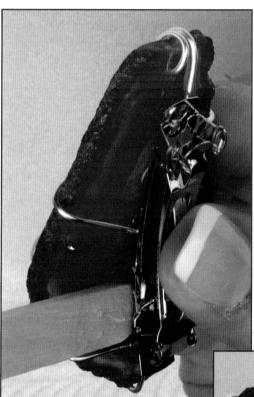

Apply more glue to the underside of the barrette clasp. Leave the project alone for about an hour to let the glue set.

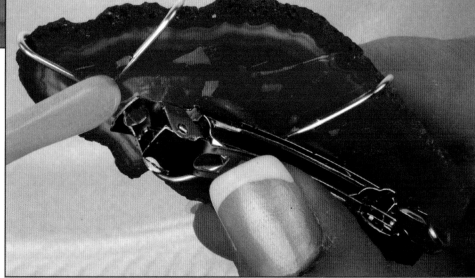

Apply a little extra glue to the crimped wire at the end that doesn't thread through the hole to keep it firmly in place. This completes the Agate Barrette Project.

Project 3
Agate Pin

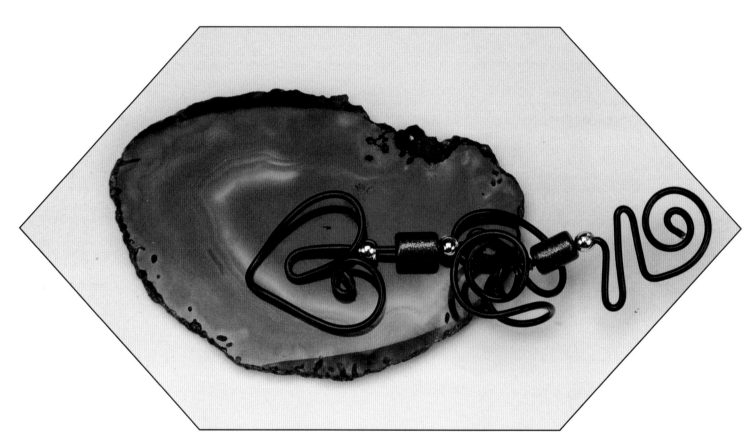

The completed Agate Pin Project.

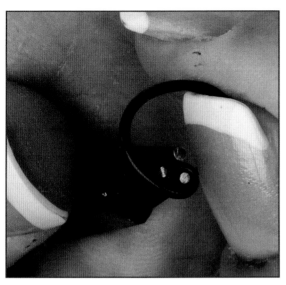

Cut a 15" length of wire. I've chosen purple wire this time to complement the stone. We'll start by creating a heart shape in wire. Begin twisting the wire as before, but this time using rounded nosed pliers. Make the first little loop as before. Then, using your thumb as a guide, begin to make the larger loop, the first curve at the top of the heart. If you don't end up with an even heart the first time you try it, do not despair. It takes some time to get wire hearts symmetrical.

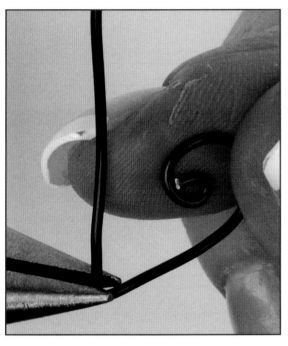

Gauge the size of the heart you want by the size of the piece you are making. Use the rounded nose pliers to make the bottom point of the heart, angling the wire up for the other side of the heart.

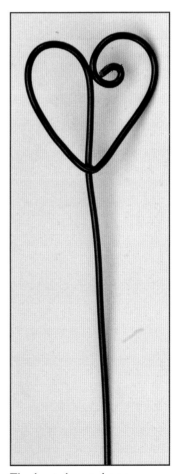

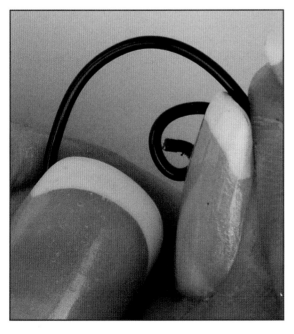

Creating the second curved loop at the top of the other side of the heart with my thumb. This is a nice, gentle curve to match the first one.

The basic heart shape is complete.

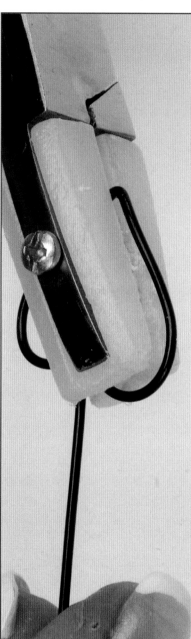
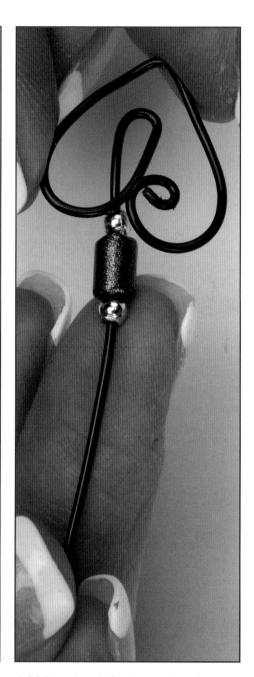

Now to add a decorative detail to the heart: take the wire extending down the back of the heart and bend it back at about the half way point. Use needle nosed pliers to bend the wire back toward the top of the heart.

Flatten or "mush" the entire wire heart sculpture at this point with the rubber tipped pliers so that the heart will lie flat against the stone later.

Add three beads for decoration at this point.

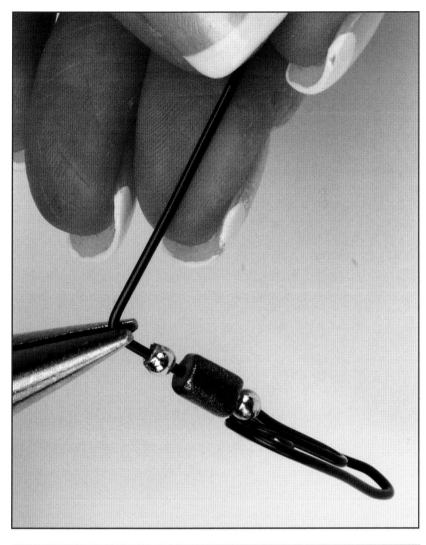

Now bend the wire at a 45 degree angle to thread the wire through the stone.

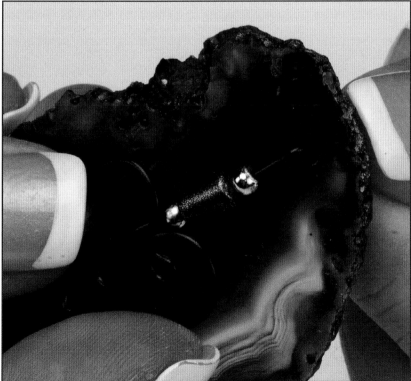

Thread the wire through the stone.

Bring the wire up around front and thread it behind the heart decoration, using the same technique as before. Remember to crimp the wire together with the pliers to keep the wire secure.

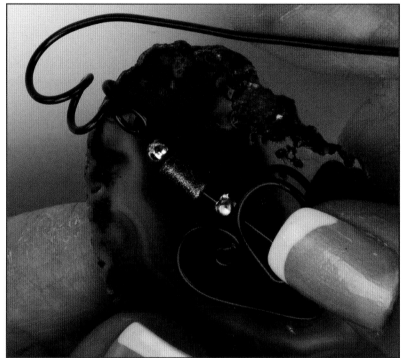

Use your thumb to create two gentle spirals to create a curlicue effect.

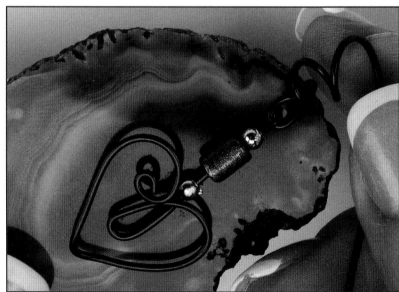

Now wrap the wire behind the heart decoration in a broad circle.

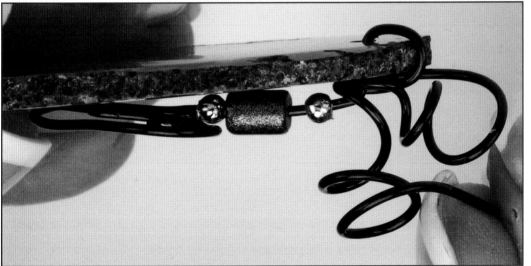

Now repeat the curlicue again, using your thumb to shape the gentle circles.

Thread the wire back up through the center of the first curlicue.

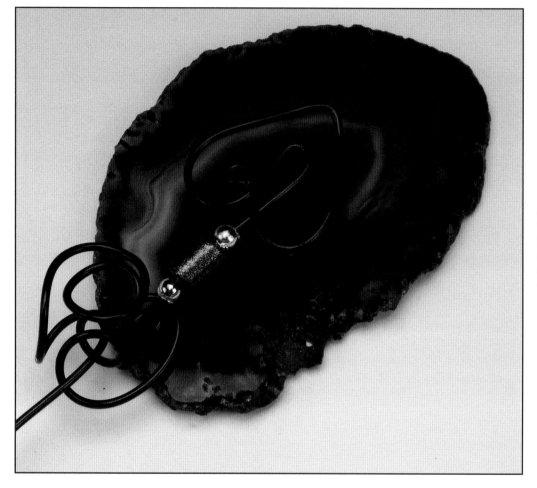

As you pull the wire through, the curlicues may change shape a bit as you see here. The curlicues flattened a bit in this case.

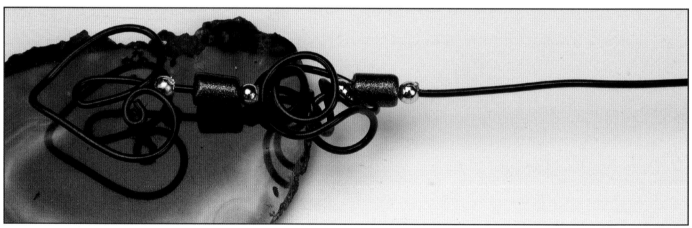

Thread three more beads onto the wire.

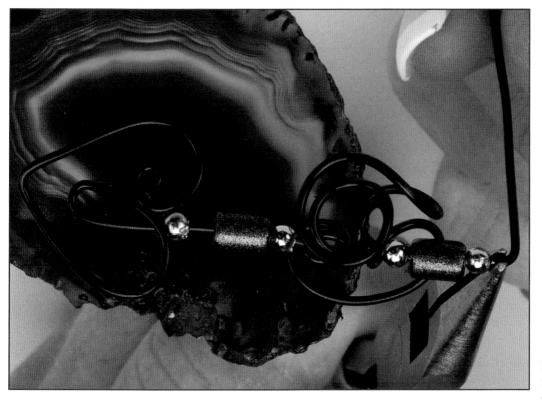

Using flat needle nosed pliers, now create a series of rounded zig-zag shape.

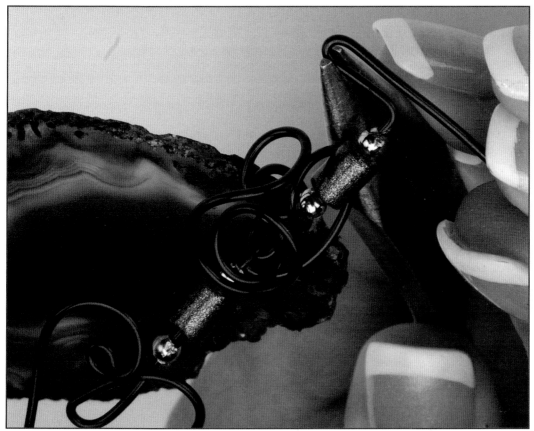

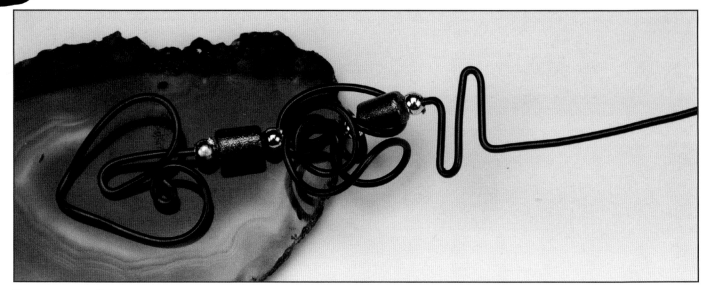

Two zig-zags will do.

Use needle nosed pliers to create a final spiral to finish the pin decoration. The wire decoration is done. Now use the Epoxy to attach the pin back to the back side of the pin.

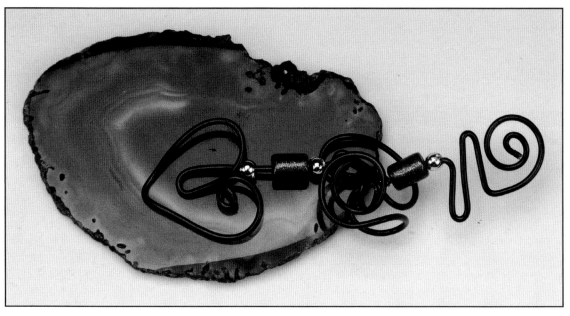

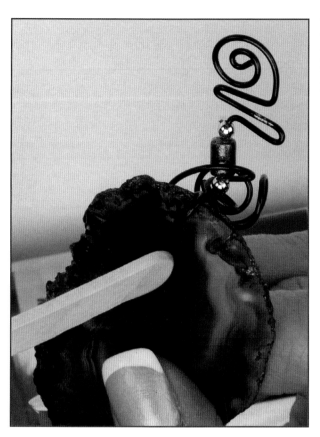

When applying glue to the back of the pin, add a bit to the hole the wire decoration passes through. This will hold the wire in place more securely.

When applying the safety pin, orient it with the hinge at the top. This way, if the safety pin comes open while you are wearing the pin, it will not slide off as readily as it would if the pin were oriented in the opposite direction.

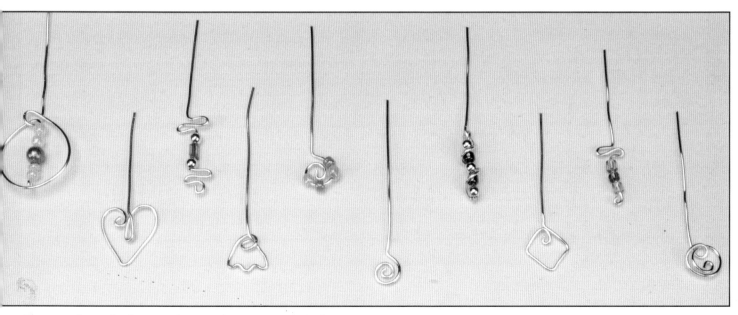

Once you have the basic technique down, you can make any number of wire decorations. These examples are more elaborate ways to begin projects for earrings, barrettes, and pins. They are also a great way to end off a wire, as in the necklace project.

Project 4
Agate Necklace

The completed Agate Necklace Project.

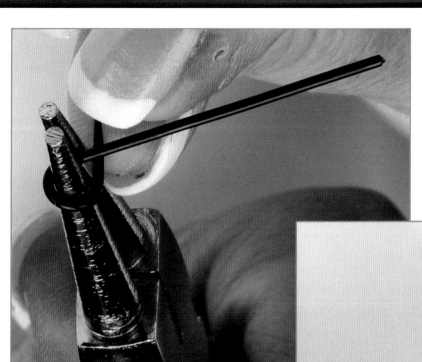

Cut 36" of wire for this project. Starting an inch down from one end of the wire, wrap the wire around your round needle nosed pliers

Using the rubber coated pliers, twist the loop twice like this.

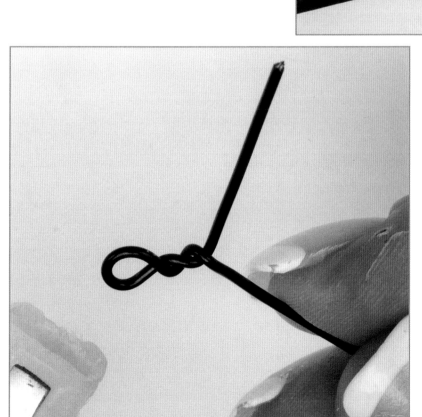

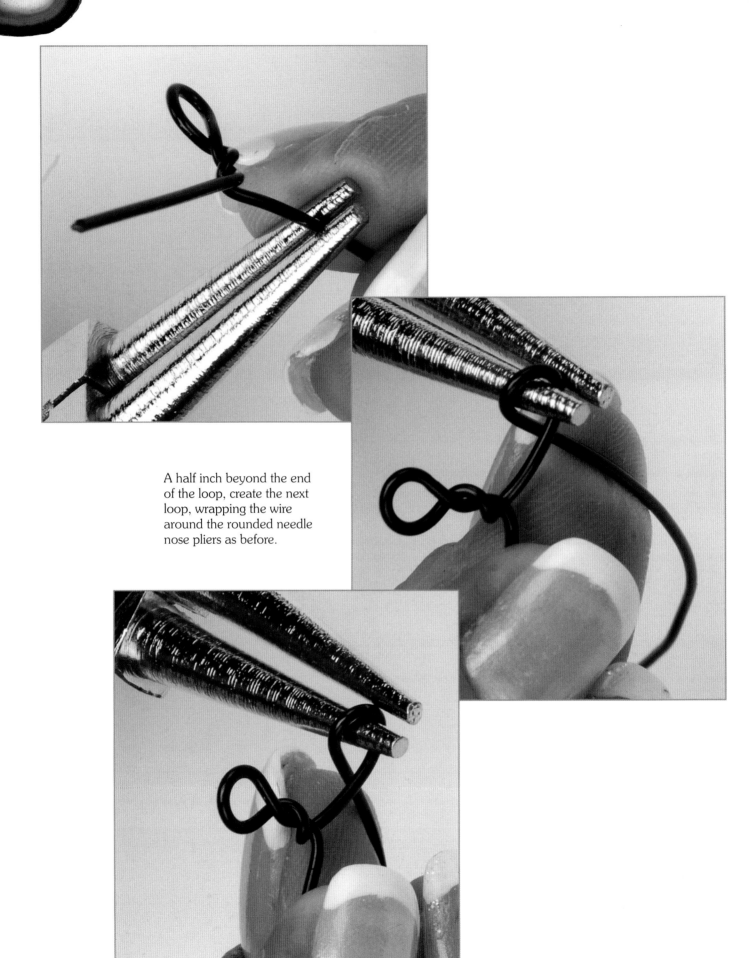

A half inch beyond the end of the loop, create the next loop, wrapping the wire around the rounded needle nose pliers as before.

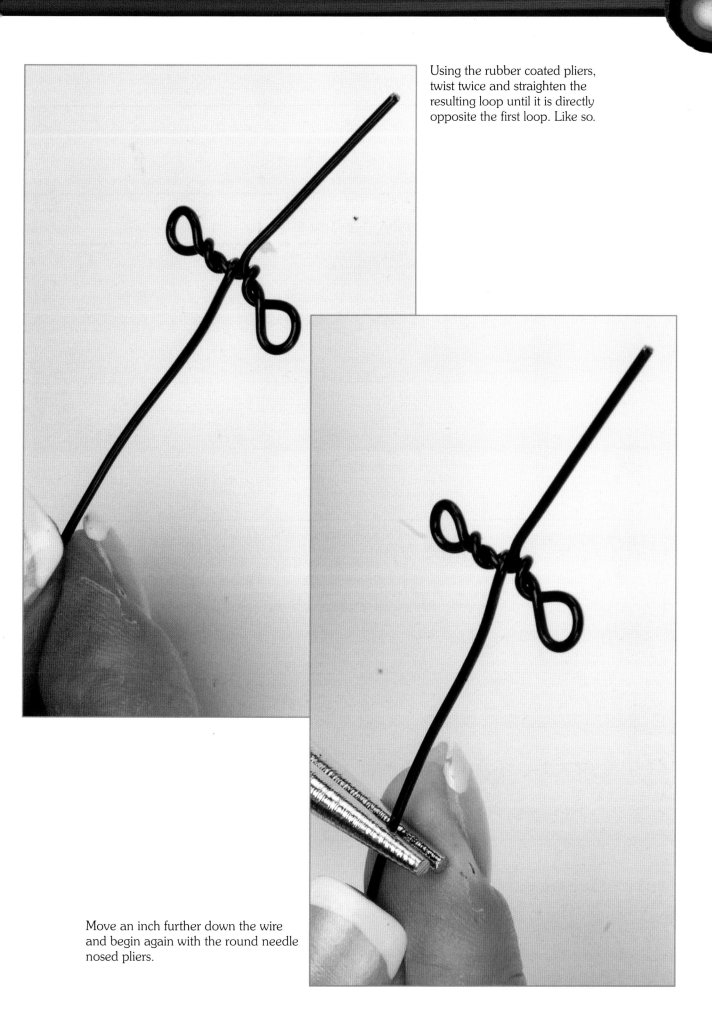

Using the rubber coated pliers, twist twice and straighten the resulting loop until it is directly opposite the first loop. Like so.

Move an inch further down the wire and begin again with the round needle nosed pliers.

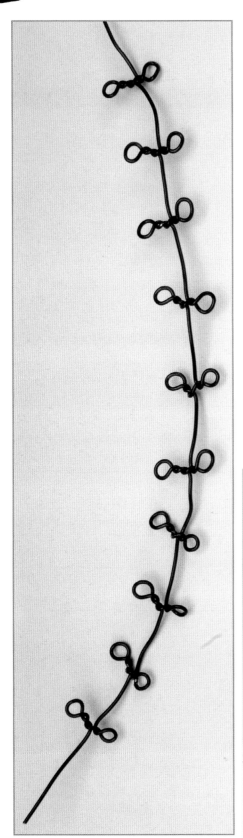

Repeat this technique. You will need enough of these to encircle your stone. You need to end up with an even number of these looped decorations.

Start wrapping the wire around the stone, one loop over the stone and the next under the stone, holding the decoration to the stone as you circle the stone.

Make sure a loop is at either end of the stone so that you have attachment points for the necklace chain.

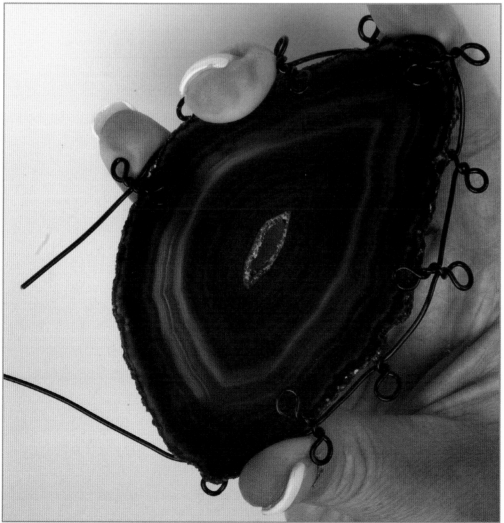

As you can see, I'm going to need two more sets of loops to finish this stone. Measure about every four sets of loops to see how many more you need.

Once you've fit the wire around the stone as tightly as you can, remembering to alternate the loops on the top and bottom of the piece, bring the ends of the wire together at the base and twist them tight.

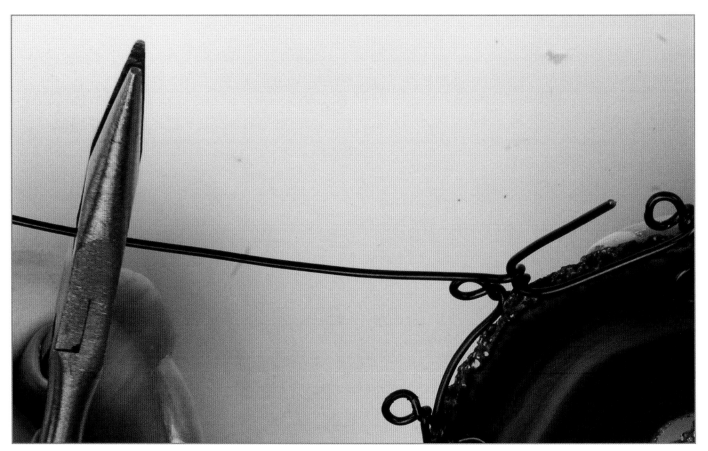

Cut off the excess wire, leaving enough for a decorative curl at the end, complete with beads.

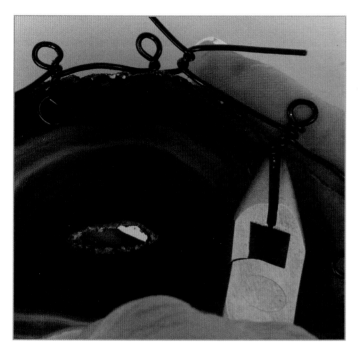

Use the needle nosed pliers now to straighten the loops to the piece all the way around. Flatten the loops to the stone as you go as well.

If there's a gap between the wire and the stone, use the needle nose pliers to tighten the wire to the stone by twisting the wire in the same direction as the loop.

Just a partial crimp will do the trick.

Cut another 36" length of wire from the spool. This we are going to use to thread through the little loops around the stone and create decorative twists and twirls with beads intermixed throughout for interest, as shown in this finished project..

Start with the same curl at the end of the second strand as we've used before and then thread the rest of the wire through the loop at the bottom of the stone.

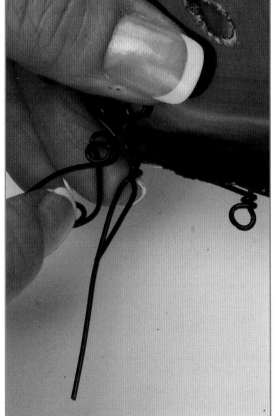

Twist the length of wire around the first loop to lock the second wire in place. This way the wire will not slip loose as you work.

Now alternate stringing a bead and twisting the wire. Add a bead and thread the wire through the second loop.

You don't have to pull the wire completely through. This is a very free form process at this point.

Wrap around this second loop and come up through the middle of the second loop, securing the loop in place.

Now add a few beads.

Pass the wire through the next loop and wrap it in place.

This is a good place for one of the curlicues.

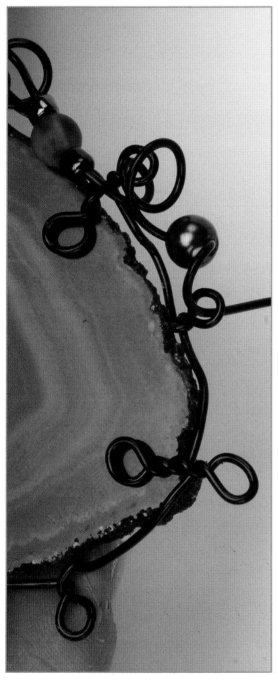

Add a bead and then thread the wire through the next loop. I have tightened the wire up to keep the curlicue shape and bead close to the stone.

Adding a few beads and passing the wire through the next loop, creating a gentle, beaded arc.

At this point, use your creativity to create interesting shapes and add beads. Keep the wire close to the stone. Think how the wire can enhance the stone with different and interesting shapes and can emphasize the shape of that stone.

The design is done and the beads are in place.

To finish off the loose ends of the wire (after twisting the ends together to secure them), add beads and curls to these end bits. If you don't wish to do so, you may also cut these loose ends away.

Like so.

Now it is time to add crimp end connectors as attachment points for the cotton cord necklace strap.

Make a broad loop using an extra piece of wire (two extra pieces of wire will be used to attach the crimp end connectors) using the needle nosed pliers. Pass this loop end of the extra wire through one the loop at one end of the triangular shaped stone. Thread the crimp end connector through the open loop of the extra wire.

Close the loop and snip off the extra wire. Curl the sharp cut edge of the wire in on itself to keep that edge from being exposed.

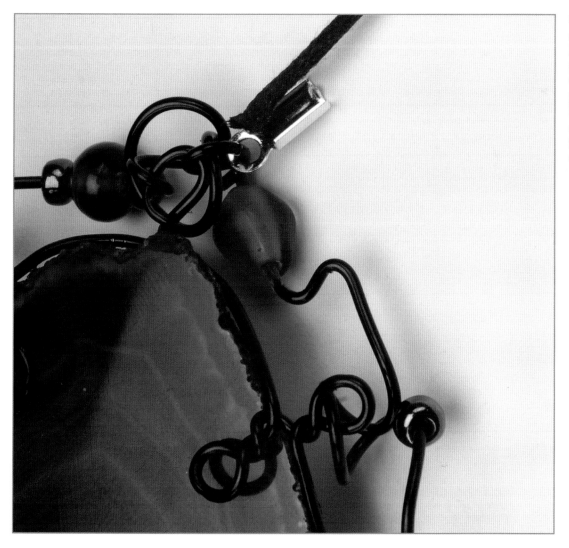

Cut a length of cord appropriate for the length of necklace you prefer. This cord will be 8" long. Two pieces 8" long will be needed. Lay the end of the cord into the open ends of the crimp end connector.

Use needle nosed pliers to close the open ends of the connector over the cord.
Repeat on the other side (refer back to photos on page 48). Both cords are now fastened to the necklace.

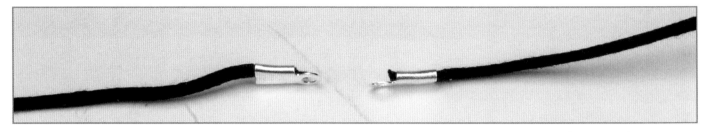

Add crimp end connectors to the other ends of the cords.

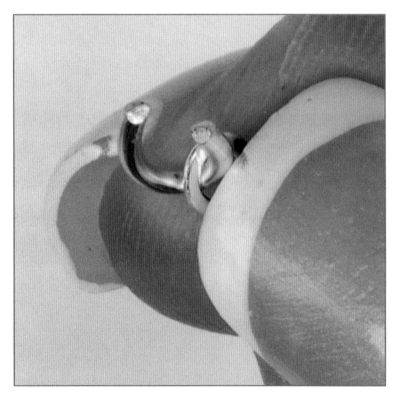

Either buy or make thin silver rings as connectors between the crimp ends connectors and the necklace clasp.

Add the clasp to the connector ring and use the pliers to crimp shut the ring. Repeat with the other cord.

The clasp is attached. The necklace is complete.

Gallery of Agate Projects

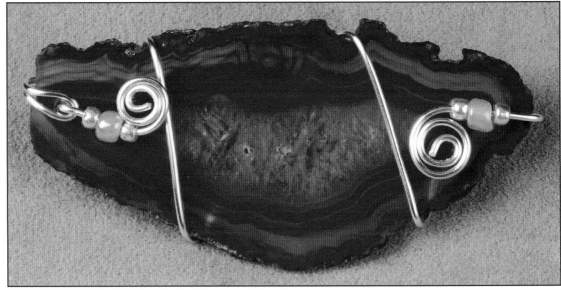

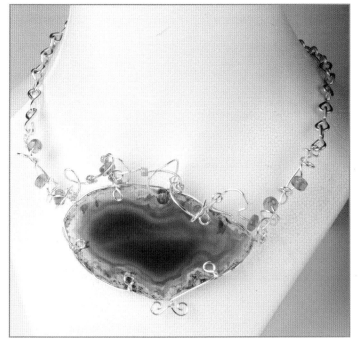

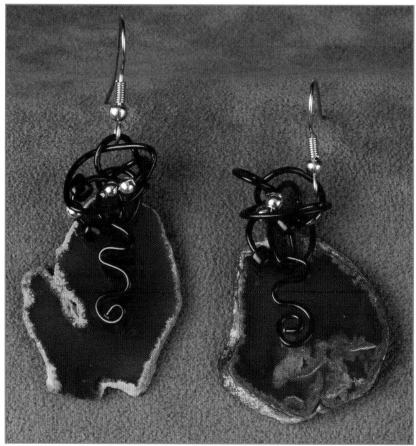

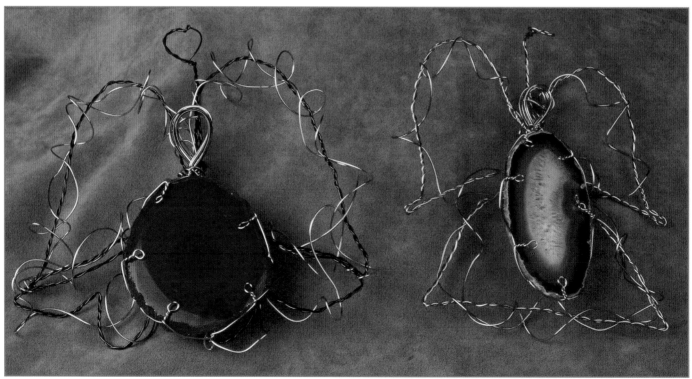

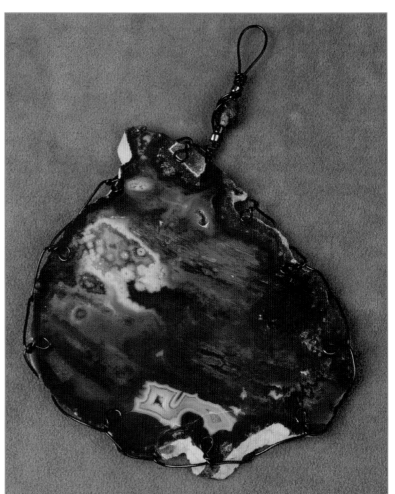

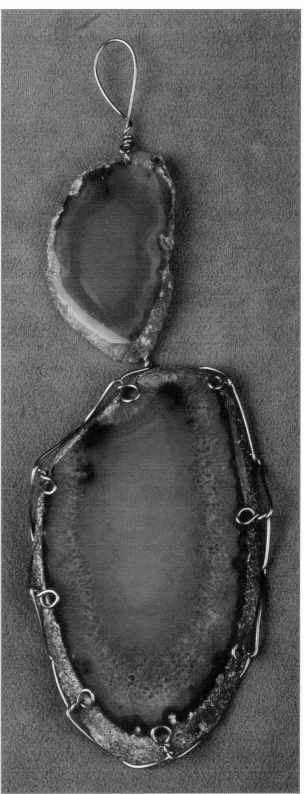

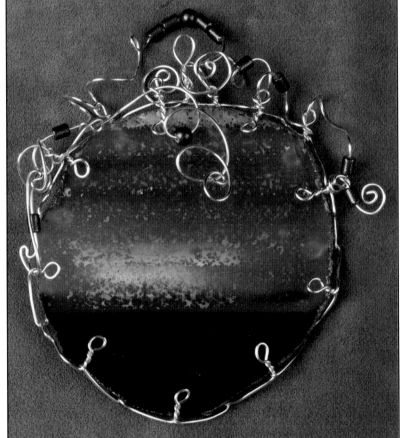

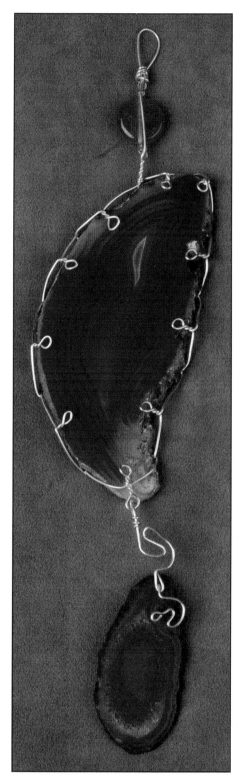

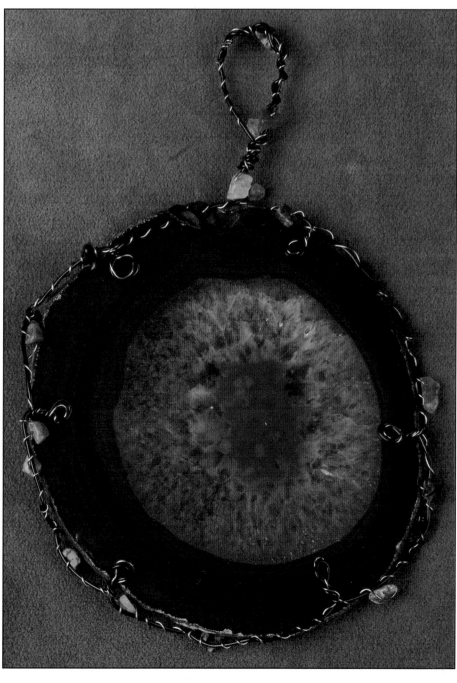

Resources

These are websites where I get my information in agates and supplies:
http://www.joellessacredgrove.com/Gems/agate.html

For the agates: http://www.pelhamgrayson.com

For the wire: http://www.parawire.com